Lead

Strategic Management and Leadership for Innovators and Solopreneurs

Ric Thompson

Ric Thompson

© 2014

All Rights Reserved. No part of this publication may be reproduced in any form or by any means, including scanning, photocopying, or otherwise without prior written permission of the copyright holder.

Disclaimer and Terms of Use: The Author and Publisher have strived to be as accurate and complete as possible in the creation of this book, notwithstanding the fact that they do not warrant or represent at any time that the contents within are accurate due to the rapidly changing nature of the Internet. While all attempts have been made to verify information provided in this publication, the Author and Publisher assume no responsibility for errors, omissions, or contrary interpretation of the subject matter herein. Any perceived slights of specific persons, peoples, or organizations are unintentional. In practical advice books, like anything else in life, there are no guarantees of income made or health benefits received. This book is not intended for use as a source of medical, legal, business, accounting or financial advice. All readers are advised to seek services of competent professionals in medical, legal, business, accounting, and finance matters.

Printed in the United States of America

Lead

Just to say Thank You for Purchasing this Book I want to give you a gift <u>100% absolutely FREE</u>

A Copy of My Special Report
"*Outsource Time*"

Go to
www.DoneForYouSolutions.com/OutsourceTime
to Receive Your FREE Gift

Table of Contents

INTRODUCTION	7
WHAT DOES IT MEAN TO MANAGE	9
PLANNING	10
LEADING	11
CONTROLLING	12
WHAT'S YOUR MANAGEMENT SCORE?	13
SECTION 1 – MANAGING THE MONEY	16
KEEPING SCORE & KNOWING YOUR POSITION IN THE LEAGUE	16
BASICS OF FINANCIAL MANAGEMENT	17
BOOKKEEPING BASICS - ACTIVITIES IN THE YEARLY ACCOUNTING CYCLE	19
MANAGEMENT EXERCISE #1: BUILD YOUR FINANCIAL TEAM	21
FINANCIAL STATEMENTS AND ANALYSIS	22
FINANCIAL ANALYSIS – WHAT THE NUMBERS MEAN AND WHY THEY'RE IMPORTANT	24
Profit Analysis.	24
SECTION 2 – MANAGING THE PEOPLE	26
DAY ONE – WHERE DO YOU NEED HELP?	27
MANAGEMENT EXERCISE #2 - DO YOU NEED A RUNNING BACK OR A WIDE RECEIVER?	29
DAYS TWO THROUGH EIGHT – DEFINING THE JOB	31
MANAGEMENT EXERCISE #3: CREATING YOUR PLAYBOOK	31
DAY NINE - STARTING YOUR SEARCH	34
Where to Look for Team Members	*34*
Outsource or Hire? Which is the Best Option for Your Business?	*35*
What is Outsourcing?	*35*
What do you Outsource?	*37*
Where do you Find Qualified Freelancers?	*39*
Hiring Employees	*40*
How to Find the Right People	*41*
DAY TEN - WRITING YOUR JOB DESCRIPTION	43
Creating Job Descriptions	*43*
Requirements for the Job	*44*
What are Your Hiring Tools?	*44*
MANAGEMENT EXERCISE #4: WRITE YOUR JOB DESCRIPTION	50
MANAGEMENT EXERCISE #5: POST YOUR JOB	50
DAY ELEVEN THROUGH FOURTEEN – INTERVIEWING	50

Interview Questions	53
Questions You Should Not Ask	56
MANAGEMENT EXERCISE #6: INTERVIEW QUESTIONS	56
DAY FIFTEEN - GETTING REFERRERS TO TALK	56
MANAGEMENT EXERCISE #7: PREP FOR REFERENCE REQUESTS	59
MANAGEMENT EXERCISE #8: INTERVIEW POTENTIAL CANDIDATES	59
DAY SIXTEEN THROUGH TWENTY-ONE – EVALUATE CANDIDATES	60
MANAGEMENT EXERCISE #9: TEST CANDIDATES/NEW HIRES	60
Management Skills	61

SECTION 3 – MANAGING THE SYSTEMS 62

SYSTEMS	62
What Systems are Important to Your Business?	62
MANAGEMENT EXERCISE #10: MAP YOUR SYSTEMS	63
METRICS	65
The Importance of Metrics	66
What to Measure	67
MANAGEMENT EXERCISE #11: CREATE WORKING METRICS FOR YOUR SYSTEMS	70

SECTION 4 - MANAGING THE DOWNSIDE AND COVERING YOUR ASSETS 73

PROTECTING YOUR ASSETS	73
Sole Proprietorship	75
General Partnership	75
Limited Partnership (L.P.)	75
S Corporation & Limited Liability Company (L.L.C)	75
C Corporation	76
Insurance	76
MANAGEMENT EXERCISE #12: INSURANCE INVENTORY	77
MANAGEMENT EXERCISE #13: GO SHOPPING	78
PROTECTING THE BUSINESS' ASSETS	78
MANAGEMENT EXERCISE #14: CONFIRM COMPLIANCE	80
US TAX LAW BASICS	80
Writing it Off: Deductions	81
Employee Taxes	82
Fun Tax Deadlines!	83
MANAGEMENT EXERCISE #15: FUN WITH TAXES!	84
CONTRACTS	84
MANAGEMENT EXERCISE #16: CHECK OUT CONTRACTS	85
EMPLOYEE LAW VS. CONTRACTOR LAW	86
MANAGEMENT EXERCISE #17: HIRE AN ATTORNEY	86

INSPIRED ACTION 89

WHAT'S YOUR MANAGEMENT SCORE NOW?	91
CONCLUSION	94
CHECK OUT SOME OF RIC'S OTHER BOOKS!!	96

Introduction

I want to thank you and congratulate you for purchasing "*Lead : Strategic Management and Leadership for Innovators and Solopreneurs.*"

Thinking back to all the jobs you've had in your life, you've probably had your fair share of managers. Some of them were probably the typical managers from Hell. Hopefully there were a few good ones in there too.

What was the difference between the good managers and the um…not-so-good managers?

Good managers are like classical music. They linger in the background, setting the pace, keeping order, uplifting, and adding value and quality to the environment. Classical music and good managers don't impose themselves.

Managing your business is more than simply hiring people and making sure they do their job. Truth is, if you hire well, you won't need to make sure they're doing their job. Management is about seeing the big picture and being the person to make sure all the facets of an operation are moving together efficiently.

If you are ready to take your business to the next level and blow past the competition, effective management is the key to making that goal a reality. Understanding how to manage your finances, your people, and your systems effectively will position you to optimize everything from your business process to your profits.

With the help of Lead, you're on your way to achieving just about anything you can imagine.

Thanks again for purchasing, I hope you enjoy it!

Ric Thompson

Lead

What Does it Mean to Manage

> *"Management is, above all, a practice where art, science, and craft meet."*
> — Henry Mintzberg, McGill University

Have you ever been in a restaurant where the manager is helping to serve the food, seating people, visiting guests, and who knows, can maybe even be found in the kitchen? This type of manager is a common scenario. They're the folks that think the role of a manger is to fill in the gaps. Actually, however, the role of a manager is to make sure there aren't any gaps in the system. The role of a manager is to plan, organize, lead, and control.

Now we beg your forgiveness in advance because we're about to use a sports metaphor. We know that can be ridiculously cliché, but it does illustrated the point. Take the coach of a football team – we're talking American Football here….

He doesn't step onto the field and throw the ball for the quarterback when the QB isn't feeling up to the job. The coach doesn't block, tackle, kick, or receive.

The coach of a football team looks at the big picture. The coach sees where improvements need to be made in communication, in execution, and in coaching – and he implements strategies for improvement.

As the entrepreneur, you're the coach of your team. You don't actually get down on the field and play the game, but you DO need to make sure your team is playing and winning.

As an entrepreneur and manager, there are four basic functions to fulfill.

They are:

- Planning
- Organizing
- Leading
- Controlling

Let's look at them in detail for a moment.

Planning

Planning is quite simply the act of setting priorities and choosing goals for the business. When you plan, you also decide how those goals will be achieved. Planning involves identifying goals, objectives, methods, resources needed to carry out responsibilities and dates for completion of tasks.

Planning can be anything from

- Planning the marketing
- Planning the staffing
- Planning projects
- Planning communications strategies
- New product planning, etc…

Examples of planning are strategic planning, business planning, project planning, staffing planning, advertising and promotions planning.

Organizing

This is a function that often trips up new business owners and managers. Organizing doesn't mean stepping in and controlling the situation. You're not an air traffic controller, you're a manager, a business owner. Remember, the team manager isn't down on the field, s/he's up in the box planning and organizing. So what does organizing mean from a management perspective?

Organizing is allocating and configuring resources to accomplish the preferred goals and objectives established during the planning processes. Organizing begins with the systems in the office, including everything from the file cabinets and organizing staff, to the organization and execution of the business plan. All of the functions of management are intertwined and dependent upon each other.

Leading

Leading is tough. It's much easier to "manage" than to lead.

> *"Effective leadership is not about making speeches or being liked; leadership is defined by results, not attributes."*
> *- Peter F. Drucker*

Leading is establishing direction and influencing people to follow that direction. It is being a motivational force, a force with an organized direction and a plan. It is the ability to inspire others to a common cause; to challenge people and then to help them reach their goals. The goal of a football team may be to win a superbowl or to have the best defense in the country, which means the coach's job is to motivate the entire team to work together to attain that goal. Motivation isn't a onetime pep talk. Motivation is an ongoing responsibility, and as part of management, it involves organizing and planning, and often restructuring, to attain the goal as a team.

Business is no different. If your goal is to launch a new product by the end of the year, the pep talk at the beginning of the year won't be enough to get the job done. You'll want to have systems in place to evaluate progress, to re-motivate, and to make sure everyone is on track – even if "everyone" is just you. If they're not, then that is where the next function of management comes into play.

Controlling

Controlling means monitoring and adjusting resources and processes to achieve goals and objectives in a highly effective and efficient fashion. This includes things like financial management, legal compliance, personnel, risk management, and feedback procedures.

Being an entrepreneur means being the leader of your team. Not only do you have to hire the right team members, you have to give them direction and goals, tools, and resources to attain those goals, as well as the desire to stay focused. It's a big job, but it's fun….

Let's get started.

Lead

What's Your Management Score?

Managing your business is not limited to managing and hiring people, though that's certainly an aspect of it. However, a true job of management is much bigger than that. Management looks at the big picture, the systems and strategies, plans, and compliance issues. We're talking about everything, from managing your money, your people, your systems, to managing the potential downside of your business.

Before we dive right into the nitty-gritty, take this evaluation. You'll retake it at the end of the guide to see what progress you've made.

On a scale of 1-10 (10 being the highest), rank where you currently stand with regard to the management of your business.

I know what areas of the business I need help with and have a plan for bringing that help in.

1   2   3   4   5   6   7   8   9   10

I know how to create comprehensive job descriptions, listings, and SOPs to assist in hiring and training new team members.

1   2   3   4   5   6   7   8   9   10

I understand the differences between outsourcing and hiring, and know which option is best for my business right now.

1   2   3   4   5   6   7   8   9   10

I'm confident in my ability to evaluate candidates for a position in my company.

1   2   3   4   5   6   7   8   9   10

I have a step-by-step system for interviewing candidates and their references.

1   2   3   4   5   6   7   8   9   10

I am confident that my personal and business finances are in order, and that I have people and systems in place to ensure they stay that way.

1   2   3   4   5   6   7   8   9   10

I know the most important systems in my business and have metrics in place to measure their effectiveness and performance.

1   2   3   4   5   6   7   8   9   10

I am confident that my personal and business assets are being protected.

1   2   3   4   5   6   7   8   9   10

I am confident that my business is compliant on all local, state, and federal tax and licensing issues.

Lead

SCORING

Add up all the numbers you circled._____

Divide the total number by 9

Record your "Management Score" here _____

Section 1 – Managing the Money

"I think the most important CEO task is defining the course that the business will take over the next five or so years. You have to have the ability to see what the business environment might be like a long way out, not just over the coming months. You need to be able to both set a broad direction, and also to take particular decisions along the way that make that broad direction unfold correctly."
– Chris Corrigan

Disclaimer – this is NOT financial advice. It is meant to give you direction when you talk to a professional. ALWAYS use a qualified accountant for financial advice.

OK – that said....

Keeping Score & Knowing Your Position in the League

Back to the sports metaphors! How on earth can you hire and plan your team when you don't know the score? Accounting and finance, as mundane as the tasks may seem to some, are vitally important. When you know the score, you know if you're winning the game or losing the game. When you know how many games you've won or lost you can chart where you stand in the league. The same goes for your business. Only score is kept in business by the bottom line – the finances.

What you put your attention on grows stronger. If you're spending time focusing on the numbers and the bottom line, they will grow stronger. So how do you focus on the score? How do you focus on the numbers, particularly when you're

Lead

busy hiring, planning, organizing, leading, and controlling? Well, you already know the answer – hire an expert. Actually, hire two experts: a bookkeeper and an accountant. Before you can do that, however, you need to know what they do.

Basics of Financial Management

The role of a bookkeeper: Bookkeepers keep complete, up-to-date, and accurate records of accounts and financial documentations. It is their job to verify and enter information into journals and ledgers or into a computer. They periodically balance the books, usually monthly, and compile reports and financial statements. Bookkeepers may also receive, record, bank, and pay out cash – accounts payable and accounts receivable. They balance checkbooks with monthly bank statements. They may also handle payroll, make bank deposits, maintain inventory records, purchase supplies, prepare purchase orders, and do expense reports.

The role of an accountant: An accountant evaluates the bookkeeper's records and shows the results in financial statements as losses and gains. Accountants must also be able to analyze a set of financial records and prescribe the system of accounts that will most easily give the desired information. They need to be able to relate the information to you so you can make accurate predictions and business decisions, and they need to be able to clarify the economic and the legal aspects of a business as well as prepare your tax returns.

It is important to have both an accountant and a bookkeeper. Why? A bookkeeper isn't an accountant. Keeping records is very different than reporting on and analyzing the records. It's like the difference between an electrician and an electrical engineer. The electrician can wire your home or business, but an electrical engineer will design the systems in your home, neighborhood, and even in your city. They look at the big picture, and so does an accountant. That being said, if you pay an accountant to do your bookkeeping, you're paying too much.

In addition to hiring an accountant and a bookkeeper, accounting software makes the job of keeping track of everything significantly easier. Imagine having years of financial data kept in journals lost. Not a fun thought, is it? In fact, it is downright frightening. This is where accounting software makes life easier – just don't forget to back up your data!

There are a number of accounting software packages designed for large and small operations. Here are a few of the most popular products:

- Quickbooks
- MYOB
- Microsoft Office Small Business
- Peachtree

When making a decision about what accounting software to use, talk to your accountant and bookkeeper. They'll have recommendations, and they'll also be able to help you set up your business on the new system.

A quick note about personal finances. It is extremely important to keep your personal and business finances separate. Why? Um....audit, lawsuit, theft.... Imagine if someone got a hold of your business AND your personal financial information because they were kept in the same system. Additionally, the federal government does not look highly upon folks who let their personal and business money cook in the same pot. Keep separate bank accounts, separate credit cards, and separate accounting systems. There's no

Lead

downside to keeping your information separate.

Basic skills in financial management start in the critical areas of cash management and bookkeeping, which should be done according to certain financial controls to ensure integrity in the bookkeeping process. New leaders and managers should soon learn how to generate financial statements (from bookkeeping journals) and analyze those statements in order to really understand the financial condition of the business. Financial analysis shows the "reality" of the situation of a business – seen as such, financial management is one of the most important practices in management. Let's take a look at the activities in the yearly accounting cycle. Note, this isn't Accounting 101 – this is a very brief introduction to how to set up your business for accounting and financial success. When everything is set up right from the beginning, it'll save countless hours and frustration later. Do it right the first time!

Bookkeeping Basics - Activities in the Yearly Accounting Cycle

Bookkeeping begins and ends with a chart of accounts. These include five basic categories: assets, liabilities, net assets or fund balances, revenues, and expenses. Each account is assigned an identifying number for use within the accounting system. In order to decide what to include in your chart of accounts, you will want to consider each of the following points:

1. Financial Controls. Every successful system has checks and balances. What systems will you have in place to make sure the accounting information is accurate? Options include regular financial audits by inside or outside parties, or keeping paper journals as well as computerized ones. Determine in advance

how to back up your accounting information. Not just the software data, your entire system. This will help prevent mistakes and potential fraud or theft.

2. Managing a Budget. For many the word "budget" is a four letter word. It implies restrictions, much like the word "diet". However, a budget is nothing more than a plan of how you're going to spend your money and like any plan, it can be revised. Budgets are critical to financial success and planning. How else will you know how much you have to spend on marketing if you don't have a working budget? Budgeting tells you how much you can afford to pay an employee or contractor, and it helps you forecast future projects.

3. Managing Cash Flow. Cash flow can make or break a business, and managing your cash flow can be one of the most difficult tasks for new business owners. You want to be able to pay your bills and continue to grow your business. The general rule of thumb is to invoice early with short terms and to pay slowly – of course, not so slowly that you risk bad credit! Talk with your accountant about optimal cash flow management strategies. Each business has its own needs and strategies.

4. Credit and Collections. AGGGHHHH!! Collecting payment from clients may be the least fun aspect of operating a business, and it's a great idea to outsource this. However, before you outsource this responsibility, have a plan in place. What are your payment policies? What course of action will you follow if payment is late? If payment is not made? Will you send letters? Phone calls? Lawyers with brass knuckles? OK... maybe not brass knuckles. What is your plan of action?

Lead

Management Exercise #1: Build Your Financial Team

Hire an accountant and/or a bookkeeper. If you already have both, make certain you have the right person for the job. Here are some basic questions to ask candidates:

- Are you a CPA? This is a question only for the accountant. You don't need a CPA for a bookkeeper.

- How many years have you been in business?

- What is your average response time?

- What is the size of your firm?

- What kind of experience do you have with businesses like mine?

- What accounting software programs are you familiar with?

- Who are your other clients?

- How do you calculate your fees?

- Why should I use you?

Once you have interviewed him or her, find out what your banker and/or attorney have to say about the accountant. With all of that information in hand decide if you're comfortable with him or her overall.

Ric Thompson

Financial Statements and Analysis

To really understand the current and future conditions of your business, you have to look at certain financial statements. These statements are generated by organizing and analyzing numbers from your accounting activities. You should understand the two primary financial statements, the Profit and Loss Statement (or Income Statement) and the Balance Sheet. You should also understand how the information helps you make financial and business decisions.

For example, let's say you need $32,000 a month to run your business. You have recurring product sales that you know will bring in $28,000 for the month. You know going into the month that you need to make up $4000 to break even. Knowing this information in advance will help you plan on how to obtain that four grand or let you know you need to cut your expenses.

Let's also imagine that you have monthly expenses that total $15,000. You know you have one client who will be paying you $26,000, but that you'll be working on their account for two months. You need to make sure that for the next two months you bring in at least $4,000 more dollars to break even.

See how knowing your financial situation, and being able to analyze the information at any given moment, can be a tremendous help to planning your future both in business and with your personal finances?

Using these reports, you can also plan major capital expenditures, expansions, or even a vacation. They'll also tell you when you can afford to hire and what type of help you can afford. The score card is VITAL.

Financial Statements – We just mentioned how important it is

Lead

to know where you stand both with your business and your personal finances. Why? The business is supposed to make you money as the entrepreneur.

To see if that is actually happening, you will need to look not only at your business' score, but your own "score" as well.

Imagine yourself in this poor guy's shoes.

Business owners quite often start out with a dream and a hefty investment. That doesn't mean the business is going to succeed. Any number of roadblocks can occur along the way. Now imagine George. He's starting a business. Let's say he is offering a cell phone service, and he has quite a lot socked in the bank – enough that he's personally funding the business, paying contractors, and the like. Now he has funds coming in, and he pays attention to those. However, he's not paying attention to his own bank account. It is slowly being drained by the ongoing expenses of the business. One day, maybe he takes a look at his bank account and panics. He sells his home and moves into a smaller one that is in town rather than on the bluff overlooking the town. Time goes by and he continues sinking money into his business, certain that a break is right around the corner. Eventually, this story has a sad ending. Personal bank accounts are depleted, contractors are laid off, and the business goes under. If only poor George had paid attention to his personal financial statements as well as his businesses.

The **Profit and Loss Statement**, also called the **Income Statement**, shows the status of your overall profits. This statement includes how much money you've earned and how much you've spent. The end result is your profits, hopefully. If you've lost money, it'll record your deficits. The Income Statement gives you a sense for how well your business is operating.

The **balance sheet** shows the overall status of your finances at a fixed point in time. It totals all your assets and subtracts all your liabilities to compute your overall net worth, or net loss. This statement is referenced particularly when buying or selling a business, or applying for funding.

Financial Analysis – What the Numbers Mean and Why They're Important

Profit Analysis.

Making a profit is the most important objective of a business. Profit can be simply defined: Revenues - Expenses = Profit. So, to increase profits, you must raise revenues, lower expenses, or both.

Break-Even Analysis.

The break-even analysis uses information from the income statement and cash flow statements to compute how much in sales must be accomplished in order to pay for all of your fixed and variable expenses. Fixed expenses are expenses that you'd have regardless of the level of sales of products or services. Variable expenses are incurred according to the level of sales of products or services, sales tax for example. A break-even analysis help you project when you'll make a profit, how much to charge for a product, or how to set a sales goal.

There are many other ratios and measures used to determine your current financial status. Your accountant should be able to give you this information quickly and easily if you need it.

Speaking of your accountant.... You now have the basics to

Lead

make sure your business is structured correctly. Your assignment is to set up a meeting with your accountant and do an analysis of your financial systems.

Here are a few things to take with you on your first meeting:

- Last year's tax returns

- Your articles of organization, if you've established your business entity

- Financial Statements

- Employee tax information

- Employee Identification Number

- Checking or banking account information

- Current accounting practices and procedures

"Hire people who are better than you are, then leave them to get on with it....
Look for people who will aim for the remarkable, who will not settle for the routine."
— *David Ogilvy*

Section 2 – Managing the People

Hiring is one of your most important responsibilities as an entrepreneur. When you hire well, it makes your job easier and your business better. Hire not so well, and you'll spend your valuable time cleaning up messes and re-strategizing to compensate for weaknesses.

Because hiring is SO important to your long-term success as an entrepreneur and business owner, this lesson is extensive. Expect to devote three to four weeks to this section. I know, that may seem like a long time, but there are several important and detailed exercises and activities which when rushed through will lose their value. Going through this process will enable you to do it over and over again as needed for the future of this or any other business you ever undertake.

To make it more manageable, we're going to eat the proverbial elephant one bite at a time.

First read the entire lesson once, then come back, and do the exercises and activities.

We're going to hire your first team member. If you're already working with an outsourced provider, or you've already hired an employee – great, you're going to bring on another one.

There is a lot to be learned from this process and doing it right will save you time and money in the long run. We're going to break this up into steps. Each step may take one day or several days. Do the work and you'll have the beginnings of a fantastic, and winning, team. Ready?

Lead

Day One – Where Do You Need Help?

Why hire?

Could you do everything yourself?

Possibly. If you want to run yourself ragged, if you don't want your business to grow, and if you enjoy stress – sure, you can do it all yourself. However, if you'd prefer to be an entrepreneur, to grow your business, and reap the benefits, then you don't have time to do everything.

Look at it this way...

Have you ever dug a hole?

When you dig a really big hole, say you're digging to plant a tree, you're standing inside the hole, and you can't tell if the hole is deep enough or wide enough. You have to get out of the hole to see the progress. If you're digging the hole yourself, that means a lot of climbing around in the dirt, in and out of the hole to see how it's going. Two people makes the job go much quicker. You have one person standing outside of the hole and one person inside of the hole digging. Three people and the job gets done all the more quickly, right? Two people digging the hole, and one person standing outside.

Now take it a step further...

As the entrepreneur, you shouldn't even be standing outside of the hole saying "dig deeper." YOUR job is to be inside planning the next phase of the landscaping. You would have hired someone to oversee the digging, someone else to dig, and maybe even an engineer to tell the diggers exactly how deep to dig the hole. Maybe the engineer would have even them the tools to measure the hole, so they didn't have to get out of it until they were finished.

So there are levels to the hiring process. Your goal is to be the most efficient, most effective team possible.

This is a very important step for your business,s but that doesn't mean it has to be stodgy or boring – so let's get to it.

Using the football team example, the coach isn't down on the field playing all eleven positions. He hires the best he can to get the job done. He hires specialists, therapists, quarterbacks, offensive linesmen, and receivers.

Putting together your own team means you now...

- Have the time you need to be able to focus on being the CEO. This is not a luxury, it's a necessity. Hiring people gives you the ability to fulfill the roles you need to fulfill to have a thriving and profitable business. True, sometimes you will be the manager, but your most important role is that of the entrepreneur. Hiring gives you the time to dedicate to growing your business, not just managing it.

- Have the time to focus on your strengths, and more importantly, to build a strong team. A company is not a single person operation (or it can't stay that way for long and succeed). Your job is to understand what strengths you need in your team and to bring them in. Do you need a strong sales team? Do you need someone who is great at public speaking? Do you need a good customer service rep? Do you need a strong office manager? If you need them, then what do you need them to do?

- Are able to take care of or supplement areas where you're not strong. For example, if you do not enjoy copywriting, you hire a copywriter. Doing it yourself is a waste of your time – no matter how important the task. Hire people who are strong in areas you are not.

Management Exercise #2 - Do you need a running back or a wide receiver?

Who will you hire first? Make sure the ego doesn't fall in here – don't hire people who make you feel good about yourself – "yes" men or women. Hire people who are GOOD at what they do and can take your business to the next level.

Step #1: Identify an area where you need help, and make a list of which tasks need to be done. What would make the biggest difference RIGHT NOW to how your business functions?

Step #2: Make a list of the tasks that take the majority of your time.

Step #3: Add any tasks you do over and over that could be done by someone else.

Step #4: Add any tasks that you do not enjoy.

Step #5: Add any tasks that you need to accomplish for your business but are not yet skilled in or familiar with.

Step #6: Look at the tasks and determine what kind of role or roles would be required to do the tasks on the list. This tells you who you need to hire as your first employee.

Step #7: Determine if you have the funds available to outsource or hire. To help determine this, consider how much time a task takes you and what your hourly value is.

Your hourly value is calculated by taking your monthly or annual profits and dividing them by the number of hours you worked in that month or year. For example, if you made $50,000 and worked 40 hours a week with no vacations then your hourly value would be $50,000/2080 or $24/hour.

Can you hire out the task at a lower rate than your hourly value?

For example, if it takes you four hours to invoice and pay your bills each week, and your hourly value is $31.25, it is essentially costing you $125.00. This is assuming that you're 100% productive when you're working, which of course no one really is. For a more accurate level of your hourly value check out the Being an Entrepreneur Guide where we provide a detailed step-by-step calculation to show you the effect of productivity on your hourly value and how to calculate it.

This calculation will tell you where it makes sense financially to pay someone else to do something. If you can hire a bookkeeper for less than your hourly value each week, then financially, it is a logical decision. Of course, the time you are freeing up needs to be spent on productive revenue-generating activities in order to make it all work.

Step #8: Now that you know who you need to hire first and what you can afford, let's create a task list for them. This is the beginning of what will be your job description and how you will know what to look for in an employee.

Lead

Days Two through Eight – Defining the Job

This section of the guide begins and ends with an exercise. This is a critical juncture in the hiring process. Do not skip this step!

Management Exercise #3: Creating your Playbook

Part One: Take a week, and document the repetitive tasks you do or the things that just aren't being handled – the things you want the new person you hire to handle.

Part Two: Map out the complete process for how something is done so you can assign it to someone else. This is called a SOP, standard operating procedure, and it works very well as a training tool.

Here's an example of an actual SOP for How to Send a Broadcast Email from the Healthy Wealthy nWise Magazine Editorial Staff – you'll see every step is laid out specifically.

How to Send a Broadcast Email

All our lists are stored in 2 separate accounts in 1Shopping Cart (1SC)

For the first account:

Go to http://www.1shoppingcart.com/login.asp

Username: ****

Password: ******

Click on "Broadcasting" bar on the left.

Click on "Manage Broadcasts"

Select the list you want to send to.

Key in the date that the email is to go out or check "Immediately" if that is necessary.

Key in the "From" – The Balancing Act uses [The Balancing Act - HWnW] in the from section.

Key in the "From Email" – The Balancing Act is from tba@healthywealthynwise.com

Pull your subject line from the template of the email (make sure you take the word "subject" out of it). Also make sure the name tag is in the proper format - <$firstname$>

Paste the body of the email into the "message section".

Make sure there are at least 10 blank lines at the end of the message – this will keep the unsubscribe link from getting in the way of the message but still make it easy to find.

Click Check this Message against the SpamAssassin™ Database link and make any adjustments it suggests to get the SPAM score below a 1.

Click "Continue Broadcast".

Give it one last check for errors in the preview pane.

Click "Send Broadcast".

Click "Continue".

Repeat the process for any other broadcasts you may have.

Lead

<u>For the second account:</u>

Once Broadcasts are scheduled in the first account log-out and re-log-in to the following 1SC account and repeat the process with the following exception:

Username: ****

Password: ******

When selecting the list you want to send to (for the newsletter choose "Entire Database")

Now it's YOUR turn.

Put together SOPs for each task that your new hire will be responsible for.

You're going to want to do each task yourself and write down each step as you go through the process. YES, this will make the task take a LOT longer than when you normally do it, but remember – this is probably the LAST time you'll have to do it!

You may want to create a new hire binder so that this information is at hand when you bring your new person on. If you're outsourcing, and your communication with your new hire is going to be primarily online, you can create a folder on your computer and email the contents to them once they've been hired.

Day Nine - Starting Your Search

Where to Look for Team Members

"Executives owe it to the organization and to their fellow workers not to tolerate nonperforming individuals in important jobs."
— Peter Drucker

In business, it is vitally important to utilize all of the tools and resources that you have available to you and to take the necessary amount of time making decisions, particularly employment decisions, before you act in order to avoid future complications and potential costly miscalculations.

Your team, whether they are outsourced contractors or full-time employees, are the backbone of your organization. Every hiring decision has potential rewards and consequences. Consider your competition. Presumably, you have access to the same supplies, equipment, and location, and other tangible aspects of your business which are more fungible.

Your strength, therefore, lies in your team. You win in today's extremely competitive economy by hiring an exceptional workforce. So where do you find those exceptional people? It depends on what type of team member you're looking for.

Outsourced workers are a fantastic way to begin. Quite frankly, there are large corporations that are run by contracted employees. You can also bring on full-time employees, or you can do a combination of both. Major corporations like Hewlett-Packard and Microsoft have thousands of contract employees and manage quite successfully. Of course, your organization may not be quite that size, yet. So where do you begin?

Outsource or Hire? Which is the Best Option for Your Business?

There are only so many hours in the day. No matter how much work you have to do, there is always more. Rather than risk your health, your sanity, and the future of your business by working 80+ hours a week, you can choose to outsource certain tasks that will help you run a more efficient, productive, and profitable business.

What is Outsourcing?

Outsourcing is essentially the hiring of contractors to fulfill different tasks and processes in your business. Outsourcing enables you as a business owner the opportunity to let go of some of the tasks that, while they may be necessary to operate your business, don't need to be accomplished by you. A great example of a tasks that are often outsourced is website design, graphic design, bookkeeping and accounting, customer service, and administrative functions.

There are many benefits to outsourcing including:

- Access to potential team members from around the world. The internet makes it possible to hire anyone from anywhere in the world. This means that it is now easier to find the right contractors at the right price. Communicating with them is as easy as sending an email or utilizing project management software solutions.

- You don't have to pay employment taxes or benefits provided you set things up properly (we'll cover this in more detail later in the guide). When you outsource, you don't have to pay benefits to your contractor because they are self-employed. It's a simple work for hire exchange.

- Increase in your hourly value. Outsourcing enables you to focus on your more profitable tasks. For example, scheduling or answering email can take a tremendous amount of time, time you could be spending with clients or developing your business.

- Saves time. Outsourcing saves you time learning new skills. We all have some skills we're strong in and other skills we struggle with or have very little knowledge of. Instead of spending days or weeks learning how to accomplish a new skill like programming, you can outsource the task to a professional and focus on your strengths.

- Have more fun. Outsourcing enables you to do what you enjoy. Rather than spend a day invoicing and updating your books, you can hire a bookkeeper who enjoys accounting and balancing your business checkbook.

What do you Outsource?

There are three categories of tasks that are generally outsourced. They include:

Administrative tasks – These are tasks like answering your emails, updating your website, scheduling, shipping, and so forth. These are generally time-consuming tasks that can easily be outsourced to qualified assistants readily available and at competitive prices.

Technical tasks – These types of tasks require a basic technological knowledge like search engine optimization or web design.

Professional tasks – Include things like accounting and legal compliance – things that a team of professionals have spent years in school to understand and more years honing their craft. Do NOT try this at home, boys and girls…

When outsourcing any project or task to a freelance individual, it is important to ask a few questions including:

- Have you handled these tasks/responsibilities before?
- Do you have references?
- How long have you been in business?
- What do you charge?
- How do you invoice/bill?
- How will you communicate with me? Email or phone
- Will you sign a non-disclosure agreement?

Start with small test projects. Be upfront that the project is a "trial period" and that you intend to give them much more business if you work well together. Then build the relationship; you want to keep your outsourcers just like you would an employee – treat them like gold. Here's an example of one of the advertisements we've used on Elance.com to attract several 'test' candidates for a writing project:

When you outsource, you're not handing over your business, you're still the manager and owner of your company. Outsourcing gives you the freedom to move your business toward a more profitable model.

Outsourcing may be the best business decision you make for your business.

Ghost Writer Needed – iPod Project plus more...

I need a good ghostwriter who can handle multiple projects for me (one involves writing 1 to 2 paragraph intros for about 950 articles and another involves writing original business articles, so please keep these projects in mind as you bid on the current small project).

I need a brief article on how to download the audio content from our website and load it onto an iPod, and then a similar set of instructions for loading the information onto a generic MP3 player.

Some of our members have all the new "toys" but don't really know how to use them – so this article will be used to help them integrate their technology with our membership info.

Please bid your "project rate" and then let me know how you handle article writing and formatting in the PMB.

Thanks and I look forward to working with you!

Lead

It can free up valuable time for you to focus on more profitable tasks, it can increase your hourly value, and it can certainly make you more productive.

Where do you Find Qualified Freelancers?

There are many tools and resources to help you find good freelancers. They include:

- Search engines – If you're outsourcing transcription, scheduling, and email tasks, you could search for a virtual assistant via the search engines and likely come up with a thousand potential candidates who own and operate their own virtual assistant or administrative business.

- Visit freelance websites – Many contract workers regularly visit and freelance job boards. For example, elance.com, guru.com, and rentacoder.com allow you to post your project or job and have individuals bid on it.

- Network online and offline – Mention your need for help on forums and associations you participate in. Tell friends and associates. Tell the people you know at school events, at your church, or even in line at the grocery store.

Hiring Employees

"The best executive is the one who has sense enough to pick good men to do what he wants done and self-restraint to keep from meddling with them while they do it."
— *Theodore Roosevelt*

Hiring, like outsourcing, is an excellent way to hand over some of the tasks of your business and the benefits are generally the same as outsourcing. However, there is one main difference.

When you hire, you will have day to day, face to face, contact with your employees. This can make it easier to communicate what you need accomplished, as well as keep track of what is being accomplished and how your employee or employees are doing with their jobs.

Some other benefits include:

- Timeliness – A staff member is likely to be a bit faster at completing assignments simply because they're on site, they work for you and have no other client obligations, and any questions they have can be answered by walking to your office and asking you.

- Quality assurance – If you're communicating via email in a language that is not your contractor's native language, as may be the case with outsourcing, mistakes and miscommunication can occur. Not to say that they can't occur when you have an employee; however, they're not as likely to happen.

- Predictable cash flow – With regular employees that receive regular paychecks, it can be much easier to predict your cash flow. Vendor prices change, and if they charge you a monthly retainer you may be paying for services that you do not need some months.

Like outsourcing, you may choose to hire people based on three different basic categories:

- Administrative tasks. Billing, shipping and receiving, customer support.

- Technical tasks. Programming and product development.

- Professional tasks. Copywriting, SEO, marketing

When you reach a certain growth point, you may also want to hire executives to run your company.

How to Find the Right People

Hiring can be a detailed process. You want to hire someone who will be skilled at the tasks you need accomplished; you want to hire someone you can trust, work with, and preferably someone you like. This will generally require some kind of screening and interviewing process. The best bet to find ideal employees is to:

- Know exactly what you're hiring for. Have a detailed job description and a list of requirements. Also know what you're able to pay and any benefits you may be able to offer your employees.

- Have a time frame in mind to fill your new job. Filling an open position is a goal. Treat it as such and develop a plan to reach your goal including when you will have the position filled.

- Be prepared with appropriate interview and screening questions.

- Hiring is a negotiation process. Remember what each party has to offer and focus on the possibility of working together.

- Where to look to find your new employees:

- Use a recruiter

- Place a Help Wanted ad

- Hire a temporary individual to test the waters

- Use your local networking contacts

Note – Before you hire an employee, visit your accountant to set up the proper payroll and tax accounts. If you don't have an accountant – hire one. It is EXTREMELY important to stay compliant with all tax issues when you have employees!

Lead

Day Ten - Writing Your Job Description

> *"When employees and employers, even co-workers, have a commitment to one another, everyone benefits. I have people who have been in business with me for decades. I reward their loyalty to the organization and to me. I know that they'll always be dedicated to what we're trying to accomplish".*
> *– Donald Trump*

Creating Job Descriptions

The first step in hiring is to define what you are looking for and what responsibilities and tasks will be handled by the person in this position. This means you will need to start by compiling a list of the job's responsibilities, tasks, and communication needs. This is partially accomplished by your SOPs. These will give you some idea of what the job entails; however, there are a number of resources available online to help you find appropriate job descriptions.

For example, if you're looking for an administrative assistant or a virtual assistant, simply searching for them online will help you find what you need. Plus, a number of REALLY big companies have already done most of the work for you. Use Google to look up descriptions other companies are using for the position you're hiring for. They'll give you a starting place for your description and also help you see if you've forgotten anything.

Requirements for the Job

This is your opportunity to be choosy. After all, you're hiring someone, and they'll play an important role in your success. Be picky here. You want people to eliminate themselves from the field so that you get only the best people. The more detailed you are, the more likely it is you'll find the person you're looking for, and the less likely you'll find tons of people you're not looking for.

Some possibilities include:

- Mental Attitude
- Business experience
- Education
- Knowledge and Skills
- Responsibilities
- Work Schedule
- Compensation and Benefits

What are Your Hiring Tools?

Résumés

A candidate's résumé is most likely your first contact with them and therefore your first impression. A résumé with a lot of errors is an instant throwaway because it implies that the candidate is careless and doesn't really care about the opportunity. Also take care to examine the sentence structure and communication style of the applicant. This may or may not be a direct indication of their own communication style if they hired a professional to write their resume, but if the sentences are incomplete or choppy and unclear, that is an unfavorable sign.

Additionally, you want to look at their employment record, and steer clear of large and unexplained gaps of employment. That's not to say that every candidate shouldn't have gaps of employment. Too many people in today's job market have experienced downsizing to realistically expect candidates to have perfect employment records.

Lastly, you'll want to examine the résumé for skills, experience, and measurable accomplishments. If they don't match your needs, then there's no need to review the résumé any further.

References

References can be valuable insight to a candidate's communication skills, motivation, leadership skills, work ethic, and much more. They can also be used to verify information on the résumé like work history, education, salary, and other background information.

The key to getting important and helpful information from a referrer is to know what questions to ask them and how to ask the questions. There is an art to it and once you learn this skill, your reference checks will turn up much more helpful information than what you may have been getting up to now.

Interviews

The interview is what most hiring managers base their decisions on and where they make the most mistakes. Traditionally, most hiring managers utilize the interview to confirm the assumption that a candidate is competent and to assess their personal compatibility with the company, often relying on gut instinct to make this assessment.

This is about as accurate an assessment as a carpenter eyeballing a measurement. You have tools – use them. We'll discuss structured interviewing and types of questions, including behavioral questions and direct questions where you ask the candidate to describe a task in detail.

Testing

There are so many testing options available to companies today. Aptitude tests, assessment tests, personality tests, motivation tests, leadership tests, and tests which are specific to each and every industry and career level. One particular online company offers more than 600 different types of tests. This tool can be a vital resource for making a solid hiring decision. Here are a few testing companies to check out:

- http://www.brainbench.com/
- http://www.saterfiel.com/
- http://www.criteriacorp.com/
- http://www.previsor.com/

Lead

Background Checks

Background checks are important for two reasons. The first reason is that you want to make sure that the information that your candidate has given you is accurate. The second reason is that you want to make sure that they are representing themselves honestly. Background checks can turn up all sorts of information, some potentially unsavory, but at least you are armed with complete information – information necessary to make good decisions for your company as a whole.

Sometimes background checks muddy the decision-making waters. For example, consider the candidate that has all of the attributes that your company desires in a candidate, but a background check turns up a check-writing fraud charge. What do you do? Tread lightly here, as there may be legal considerations. Whatever your hiring decision would be in this case, it is definitely better to have the knowledge than to find out after you've made them a part of your business family.

Background Investigations

It should be noted that background investigations are very different from reference checks. Background investigations serve to verify facts already presented by the candidate. They can be as simple as you calling the educational institutes and past employers listed to verify dates, or they can be more thorough. There are companies available to hire that can fulfill this need for you confidentially, and the reports can include the following:

- Social Security Number traces

- Driver's License searches

- Education and Employment Verifications
- Misdemeanor/Felony Conviction records
- Supervisor Interviews
- Credit Reports
- Bankruptcy Records
- Federal Tax Lien Records
- Civil Litigation Searches
- Professional License Verifications
- Worker's Compensation Indices
- Reference Interviews

While this may seem like overkill for some positions, for others like a Chief Financial Officer they can be completely justified. After all, you're entrusting them with a lot of responsibility and valuable information. Always inform a candidate that you are going to be performing an investigation.

Learn from the unfortunate situation that another company had to deal with. As they should have, the company informed a candidate that was applying for a senior management position, who looked great on paper and interviewed quite well, that they were going to perform a background investigation on him. He agreed, and they began the process through a separate provider. They found out that

Lead

the candidate had a felony assault charge on his record. Apparently he had anger management issues. They decided not to hire him.

Here are a few companies that provide background checks to employers:

- http://www.employeescreen.com/
- http://www.easybackgrounds.com/
- http://www.infolinkscreening.com/infolink/default.aspx
- http://www.infocubic.net/

Test, Test, Test

Type "employee testing" into any search engine and you'll get about 25,000,000 hits. Why so many? Because employee testing is valuable to hiring managers in any industry, and because employee testing can be designed for specific industries, titles, behaviors, skills, experience levels and much more. One site, Brainbench, offers more than 600 assessments.

Testing can evaluate whether or not a candidate is capable of accomplishing the job's responsibilities. It can tell you whether or not their leadership skills are on a par with your needs. They can tell you where the candidate is most motivated, where his or her interests lie, and if your candidate is going to stick around for the long haul or jump ship when the next best thing appears.

Testing not only provides you with an unbiased measurement of a candidate's competencies, but it also enforces and validates your hiring decision. Don't let this valuable tool pass you by.

Now that you've had an overview of both outsourcing and hiring, choose which method you want to go with for the position you chose to fill.

With that in mind you're now ready to...

Management Exercise #4: Write Your Job Description

Now that you're ready to begin hiring, write your job description as you would post it in an advertisement or job bulletin posting.

Management Exercise #5: Post Your Job

Decide where the best place would be to post your opportunity. If you're hiring an outsourced employee, check the freelance websites or relevant forums or job boards. If you're hiring an internal employee, consider using one of the job sites like Craigslist or Monster.com.

Day Eleven through Fourteen – Interviewing

> "In the end, all business operations can be reduced to three words:
> people, product and profits. Unless you've got a good team,
> you can't do much with the other two."
> – Lee Iacocca

Lead

Finding the right person for the job can feel overwhelming, but you still need to select the right person for the job. An integral part of the hiring task is interviewing candidates. Interviewing is the time where most companies rely on "gut instinct." They assume that the candidate is qualified for the position when what they should be doing is evaluating their qualifications during the interview. In addition to direct questions, the interviewer should prepare specific behavioral questions, knowledge questions, and questions to assess a candidate's interpersonal skills.

The best way to conduct an interview is to have a structure established before the candidate arrives or before you get on the phone. This enables you to maintain control of the interview and to extract all the necessary information that you need to make an appropriate and effective hiring decision.

An interview structure might look like this:

- Greeting
- Brief conversation to set candidate at ease
- 5-10 warm up questions
- 10-20 Behavioral questions
- Confirmation questions. Clarify concerns.
- Candidate question period
- Closing questions/discussion. Ask for references.
- Address the next steps in the process.

- Handshake/Goodbye

- Move on to next interviewer or process is complete

Decide in advance how long you have for the interview and make sure that the candidate is aware of that time frame when you make the appointment. Also decide how you want to document the interview for later reference and in the event that any legal concerns arise. The best way to conduct any interview is to prepare ahead of time. Let's begin with questions to ask yourself about how to establish a structure.

1. Who is conducting the interview?
2. How many people are going to be interviewed?
3. What will the interview format be?
4. Series (will there be a series of interviews)
5. Face to face (or via phone) with one person
6. Sequential (the interviewee will meet with several people one after the other)
7. Group interview (several candidates meet with interviewers in a group setting)
8. How much time will you allow for the interview?
9. Lastly, what questions will you ask the candidate?

Once you've established a general format for the interview, the next step is to identify key questions that you want the candidate to answer. There may be additional questions that you'll need to ask based on the candidate's answers and there may be fewer questions that need to be asked based on the candidate's answers and performance during the interview. (If the candidate blows the interview in the first five minutes then there is no need to prolong the agony. Simply cut the interview short, gracefully, and move on.)

Lead

Interview Questions

A great place to begin any interview, after the initial introduction, is with a job description and some general rapport-building questions to set the applicant at ease. General questions might include the weather, a big sports game last night, whatever....

Next, you'll want to move in to the introductory questions. These questions serve to warm up the applicant and get them into 'interview' mode. Questions might resemble the following:

"Please describe your current job responsibilities."

"What do you like most about your current job? Least?"

"Why do you want to leave your current position?"

Based on the candidate's answers to your questions, you'll likely have a few more questions to dig deeper or clarify their answers. Then it is time to move into the competency-based questions. Competency-based questions are designed to keep the interviewer in control of the interview. They cover measurable skills, knowledge, behavior, and interpersonal skills. They are the core of the interview and where you will derive the majority of your decision making information.

The six questions you need to ask are:

- "Tell me about an unpopular decision that you've had to make and how you handled it." ---This question assesses the candidate's decision-making skills.

- "Describe a situation where you were overwhelmed by a problem at work and how you handled it." --- This would address the candidate's problem-solving skills.

- "Tell me how you prioritize tasks and budget your time?" --- Time management.

- "Tell me about a time when your team or department did not meet expected goals. How did you handle that?" --- Management or Team building.

- "Tell me about a time that you had to deal with a difficult employee/co-worker."

- "Describe what motivates you at your current job?"

A competency is a trait or quality that contributes to a candidate's ability to meet the job requirements as established by you prior to posting the position. The questions therefore focus on having the candidate explain past experiences to predict future behaviors. Questions should be designed to assess all behaviors, skills, and experiences necessary to perform the job's responsibilities.

The next stage of a structured interview is the clarification or confirmation stage. Here you briefly address questions about the candidate's education and work history, making sure to inquire about any inconsistencies. If the competency portion of the interview has been comprehensive, then this portion of the interview should be brief.

Lead

The last phase of the interview is the closing. This is where you turn the interview over to the candidate to ask any questions that they may have about the position and to establish a method of communication for the future. What is the next step? When will you have a decision made? How and when should the candidate contact you? This is also the time where salary requirements should be clarified.

Once you've completed the interview, if you haven't documented or assessed the candidate's answers to your questions, then take a few moments to record your assessment. We recommend a formal interview format where assessing an answer to a question can be as simple as circling a number on a scale of 1-10 so that you don't have to write down complete answers. This also enables reassessment of the interview to be an easier and more efficient process. Leave room at the bottom of the form for comments. Sign and date the form and make sure that the candidate's name is on the top.

Questions You Should Not Ask

There are, of course, questions that you need to avoid asking for legal and moral reasons, including questions about the origin of a name, questions about a person's residence, age, physical appearance, marital status, children, religion, and finances. Tread lightly when inquiring about education, military experience, organizations, disabilities, criminal offenses, citizenship, and a person's name, sticking only with the facts.

Management Exercise #6: Interview Questions

Based on your job description, write down a list of questions that are important and relevant to the position.

Day Fifteen - Getting Referrers to Talk

We're going to operate under the assumption that your candidates have given you qualified, quality referrers and that you're not calling their brother, mother, lawn care provider, grocer, or priest. If it weren't so common for people to give inappropriate referrers, it'd be funny.

References, whether you're hiring a freelance or contract worker or hiring someone in-house, can be an extremely valuable tool for confirming a candidate's strengths and addressing concerns and weaknesses. They are an art form because you want to extract more information from the referrers than verifying dates of hire and confirming facts. You want to ask open-ended questions that allow for insight into the candidate's qualifications.

You'll also want to make sure that you speak with at least two, preferably three, referrers and that they are a mixture of

Lead

employers or supervisors, co-workers, and employees. Additionally, it eliminates a potential bias if the referrers are from more than one employer.

Like the interview, preparation is key. Develop and write down questions to address, making sure to not only inquire about competencies but also any areas of weakness. Also utilize questions to confirm strengths. Utilizing a reference check form can help keep you on track, document responses, and serve as a valuable tool to refer to when making a final decision. Like the interview form, write the candidate's name on the top as well as the referrer's name and the date that you spoke with them.

With each reference, it is important to gradually ease into the questions and not begin with, "Would you hire this person if you were in my position?" Begin the questioning with the following questions, or a derivation of the following questions as they relate to the position:

(Keep in mind these questions are written with an employee reference in mind. Modify them as needed if you are checking references of a potential outsourcer or vendor.)

1. How do you know the candidate?
2. How long have you known the candidate?
3. During that time, what was their job title?
4. What were their job responsibilities?

Like the interview, once the referrer is warmed up, you can begin to move into more probing questions.

For example:

1. How would you describe the candidate's overall performance?

2. How productive was the candidate on the job?

3. How would you describe their attitude?

4. Did they have supervisory responsibilities? If yes, how did the candidate handle them?

5. What were the candidate's strengths? Weaknesses?

6. Where do you think the candidate could have improved?

7. How would you compare his/her performance with others that have performed the same job?

8. What do you think motivated him/her?

9. How would you describe his/her ability to work effectively with others?

10. How would you describe the candidate's management style?

11. Describe communication style and skills.

12. How would others assess the candidate's ability to perform their job?

Lead

You can then move into professional growth questions or end it here with the "would you hire this candidate if you were in my position" or "would you rehire this candidate" type question. Be sure to ask if there is anything that the referrer would like to add, and thank them for their time.

If the referrer is a past employer and is hesitant to answer any open-ended questions due to "company policy," then this should be a red flag for you. Presumably the candidate asked this person to be a referrer and they agreed – therefore they should be not only willing but eager to speak on behalf of the candidate, not hiding behind company policy. You might want to ask the referrer if your candidate asked him to be a referrer and confirm that he or she did in fact agree.

Management Exercise #7: Prep for Reference Requests

Based on your candidates, the job description, and your specific requirements, write down a list of questions to use when talking to referrers.

Management Exercise #8: Interview Potential Candidates

Based on responses to your advertisement or job posting, talk with a few candidates. Interviews don't have to be in person anymore. However, it is often helpful to talk with them on the phone. Schedule interviews and check references on the candidates you're interested in.

Day Sixteen through Twenty-one – Evaluate Candidates

> *"Organizations where people continually expand their capacity to create the results they truly desire, where new and expansive patterns of thinking are nurtured, where collective aspiration is set free, and where people are continually learning how to learn together."*
> – Peter Senge, *The Fifth Discipline: The Art and Practice of the Learning Organization*

Okay, ready?

You've gone through the steps to hire an employee. If you haven't actually taken the steps, go back, and using your exercises and worksheets go through the process of hiring an employee or a contractor. This is an important activity.

Management Exercise #9: Test Candidates/New Hires

Test your new hire or potential candidates for the position. Give potential candidates a small project. TEST them, don't take their word. Hire several candidates to do a small test project. You get to see how they work, if they deliver on time, and if they truly understand what you want. Based on the results of the test, you can then make a decision about which person is the right one for the job. This works particularly well with writers, editors, graphic designers, researchers, web designers, even nannies – it really works for ANYTHING.

This testing strategy is an exceptional tool to find not only the person who is best qualified to do the job, but also the best person to work with and communicate with you and your other team members. You can have the best quarterback in the world, but if they don't get along with the rest of the team, they may not be the right person for the job. Testing gives you the ability to evaluate all of the skills required to fill your position. It may take a little extra time, but the end result will be a finely oiled team – which means a better business and more profits.

Management Skills

This is the point where it may be good to pause and take a deep breath. Hiring an employee is heavy lifting for sure. Pull yourself out of the process and take a look at how it went. Take some time to reflect and write down some notes about how your hiring process worked so that you can improve the process for next time. Ask yourself what worked well? What would you have done differently? What are you going to do moving forward?

Section 3 – Managing the Systems

This lesson is another biggie. Approach it like you approached the hiring section. Go through the entire lesson, and then go back, and systematically work through the worksheets and exercises. When you've completed this lesson, you'll have a full-scale operating plan for your business as well as the tools to measure your success. For example, you'll have a plan for customer service and the tools to measure the effectiveness of your customer service strategy and team. You'll have systems and metrics.

> *"Checking the results of a decision against its expectations shows executives what their strengths are, where they need to improve, and where they lack knowledge or information."*
> – Peter Drucker

Systems

Systems are like the "special teams" of the football team. They make up the overall team, but each has a different set of responsibilities and duties to carry out. Just the same, a business is made up of an integrated set of systems.

What Systems are Important to Your Business?

It is important to determine what systems your business currently has and what systems it needs to function optimally. Map out the possibilities. A mind map or process map is a great way to start. Both of these mapping strategies will help link systems together and show the big picture.

Lead

Some possible systems are:

- Marketing
- Sales
- Product creation
- Product development
- Purchasing
- Production
- Customer service
- Producing a newsletter
- Billing and getting paid
- Really just about anything and everything

Management Exercise #10: Map Your Systems

Identify the primary pieces of your business and map them out. This will not only help you structure your business in the most efficient manner, it will also help you see how the systems are related and dependent on each other. It will also help you make educated decisions about improving your business.

Here are some examples to get started with. A simple customer service system. Answer the following questions.

It doesn't have to be in paragraph form. You can draw a flowchart, an outline, or a simple diagram.

- What happens when a client calls in?
- What happens if they email?
- What happens if they fax?
- Are there common reasons they contact you?
- Billing issues? If so where do they go?
- Technical support? If so where do they go?
- Product questions? What happens next?
- Need to make an appointment? What happens next?

If none of this is documented, then how can it be taught to someone else?

Here's another system example – a process flow. This one is for the client path of a book launch marketing campaign

Lead

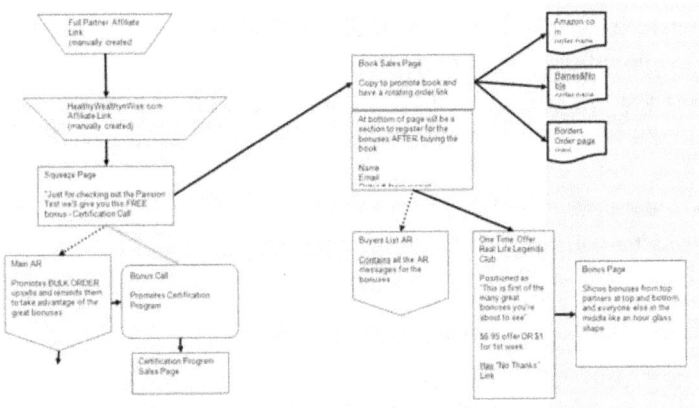

Systems are a fantastic way to create order in a business. They're like the offensive and defensive plays in a football playbook. However, how do you know if the plays are working? A football coach uses statistics. How many complete passes? How many running yards? How many quarterback sacks? In business you too need something to help evaluate whether your systems are working.

Metrics

Metrics are the little scores which make up the big score of the bottom line. Metrics let you know if your special teams are functioning properly. To keep the football analogy running: In football there are the yards rushing and passing, the kicking yards per attempt, field goals attempted and made – the list goes on. And it's from looking at all the stats – these metrics – that the coaches can see where they need to work with their players to improve. For example, running yards made by a receiver are an important measurement. They reflect the speed and capability of the receiver. If the numbers are short of goals then the coach can work specifically with the receiver to improve. Same thing for a quarterback: passing yards and running yards, in addition to completed passes, interceptions and touchdowns, are important statistics. When numbers are low, the player and the coach can specifically address methods to improve.

We just applied it to football – now let's bring it full circle to apply to your business.

The Importance of Metrics

Definition: Metrics enable you, as the entrepreneur and the manager, to evaluate whether or not your systems are working. In order to do this, the metric must be defined to detail what it is measuring. For example, customer service is a system, and a metric may be "return customers who've filed a complaint." This creates a definition of what you consider to be the customer service goal.

Measure: Metrics give you something to measure. Using the example above, if your goal is to have 75% of all customer service complaints come back for repeat business, the metric enables you to determine if you're meeting your goal. If only 50% of the customers are repeat customers you know that the system needs improvement.

Improve: Speaking of improvement, once you have a tool to measure success, you can analyze the results and plan for success. If your customer service team has a 50% success rate, you can analyze the process and find ways to improve the system.

Lead

What to Measure

Measurements can be as simple or as complicated as you make them. The important thing to remember is to make sure you're measuring information that will help your business improve, grow, and be successful. A measurement is only as useful as the information it provides. For example, a football team has an abundance of statistics they track. However, they probably don't track how many times the quarterback has a good game if his girlfriend or wife is in the crowd. The fans take care of that, right? <g> Realistically, that isn't a helpful statistic. Likewise, some information will be helpful to your business, and other information won't.

Scorecards, dashboards, and reports: In addition to various measurements, these are also different ways of looking at and analyzing the information.

Scorecards are a balanced analysis technique designed to translate an organization's mission statement and overall business strategy into specific, quantifiable goals and to monitor the organization's performance in terms of achieving these goals. It looks at four key areas: financial analysis, customer analysis, internal analysis, and learning and growth analysis. A balanced scorecard breaks broad goals down into vision, strategies, tactical activities, and metrics. It is a structured system and doesn't leave much room for variance. As an example of how a scorecard methodology works, consider an organization that has a goal to maintain employee satisfaction. This would be the vision. Strategies for achieving that vision might include approaches such as increasing employee trainings. Tactical activities undertaken to implement the strategy might include an annual "professional development" allowance. Metrics could include measurements of the number of employees who actually use their allowance, and how that ties back to their overall satisfaction and performance.

A dashboard works much the same way a scorecard does, but it is generally a single sheet of paper with all of the appropriate metrics on it – so you can basically manager the company at a glance.

Reports take the process to an even more finite level and analyze a specific system rather than the entire business. Regardless of the system or systems used to track the metrics you will need to identify and define your measurements, otherwise known as Key Performance Indicators or KPI.

Key Performance Indicators tell you how your business is operating. Before you can use them, you need to choose them. Yep, you define your key performance indicators.

Here are a few questions to ask yourself:

- What question are you trying to answer? For example, how effective is our customer service team?

- Who does this question apply to? For example, the customer service representative.

- Why is the question important? What will you do with the information? For example, it will help you determine if you've implemented the optimal customer service strategy.

- Where does data reside to answer this question? In order to measure, you have to know where you're going to get the information. In this case, the information may already exist in the customer service log and in the log that records purchases. What needs to happen is to have a system to collect and integrate this information.

- What further questions could this metric or KPI raise? Once you know how many customers come back after issuing a complaint, it may bring up additional questions such as "Why don't they come back?" "What factors play a role in a return customer?"

- What actions or decisions could be taken with this information? For example, would you hire different customer service representatives, change your policy, or offer incentives to return customers?

- The specific measure. What specifically are you measuring? It is important to know this before determining goals. If you're measuring how many customers come back after complaining, then make sure that's exactly what you're measuring.

- Use the SMART system. Specific, Measurable, Attainable, Repeatable, and Timely. You already know the system – apply it to your metrics and you'll be on a winning team!

Here's an example of an effective KPI for a retail store:

Title of KPI: Customer Retention.

Defined: The total of the number of customers who make repeat purchases in 12 months' time as a percentage of the total customers within that same 12 months.

Measured: The POS contains records of each customer. The customer information is stored and reports can be run resulting in real time information and statistics. We will run the report monthly over the course of a year to determine the percentage of return customers.

Target: Increase customer retention by 5% per year

Management Exercise #11: Create Working Metrics for Your Systems

Using the list of systems you created at the beginning of this lesson, go back and create measurable metrics and a system for tracking them. Start with the primary system of your business – the one that is most essential to your operations. This process will probably take several days. It isn't necessary to do it all at once, in fact it may be easier to do an initial rough draft of thoughts and ideas and come back to it a day or two later. It's not always easy but it must be done to track the productivity of the different systems.

When establishing metrics it is important to:

- Define your measurement

- Define your calculation

- Describe how the measurement will be interpreted

- Describe the data collection process

- Who

Lead

- What
- Where
- When
- How
- Track and analyze your measurements and results

This "system" of establishing metrics and key performance indicators helps to ensure you're measuring relevant and useful information, and it makes sure that whoever is doing the measuring is following the expected procedure.

Ask yourself the following questions to help create metrics for each system:

How do I know when this system is working? For example, with customer service, it might be the amount of time it takes for a client's question to be answered, or it could be how long a person is on hold, or how many rings before the phone is picked up.

How is the information measured?

How is the information helping you perform?

Who will compile the information and when?

How often do you look at the numbers?

Frequency is important. For example, in the customer retention example earlier, looking at the information on a monthly basis is critical to analyzing trends. Maybe customers are more likely to be repeat customers during certain months. If the information is only reviewed quarterly or annually, you'll miss out on that important variable.

Take the time to wrap this lesson up completely. The systems and metrics of your business are the key to running an efficient and productive business – all of which are directly related to your profits! Systems and metrics are the plays and stats of your business. They tell you which plays to run to make the most of your teams' skills and strengths. The statistics or metrics tell you which plays or systems are working and which systems need to be reworked. They're the key to an efficient, productive, and well-oiled team – especially once that "team" consists of more people than just you.

Lead

Section 4 - Managing the Downside and Covering your ASSets

Disclaimer – this is NOT legal advice. It is meant to give you direction when you talk to a professional. ALWAYS use a qualified attorney for legal advice.

> *"The leading rule for the lawyer, as for the man of every other calling, is diligence. Leave nothing for tomorrow which can be done today."*
> – Abraham Lincoln

To carry on with the football metaphor, this section is for making sure you're playing by the rules, making sure there are no major penalties, flags on plays, or team members booted out of the game. It is also for making sure you as the team owner are protected from the liabilities of the actions of players, managers, and crazed fans.

This is the CYA section of the guide…

Protecting YOUR ASSets

Football players use pads and helmets. Entrepreneurs use entity structuring, contracts, insurance, and more. Limiting your personal liability and protecting your personal assets from business liabilities and attacks is vital for your well-being, both personal and business. Entity structuring is the use of limited partnerships, limited liabilities, and corporations. These can help you accomplish three things:

1. Protect your assets so that sue-happy people aren't getting your livelihood and your house and car.

Seriously, if you don't separate your business and your personal identity, they can come after both and snatch them away.

2. Significantly reduce your taxes. Not establishing a business entity could result in paying a LOT more than you fair share of taxes. Now why on earth would you want to do that?

3. Protect your privacy. One of the reasons many business owners establish a separate business identity is simply to keep their private life private. You don't want your home address attached to your business where any old Tom, Dick, or Harry can look you up.

Here's a little story to really drive the point home. Louise grew up with the family boat business. She bought and sold boats. As the business grew, she made the decision to expand. She opened a marina, a storage facility, repair services, and a boat showroom for the fancy boats – the really big-ticket items. She did well, she knew her business inside and out, and she made a significant amount of cash. However, that didn't stop the police from coming in and shutting down the entire business simply because she was missing a few licenses and business registrations.

Quite simply, she didn't have permission to be doing the business she was doing. The city had her business shut down before Louise could make a phone call. She lost everything: all of her personal assets and the business.

Lead

Here are a few of the business entity options:

Sole Proprietorship

A sole proprietorship is the easiest kind of business to form and manage. The owner runs the business in his or her own name and has full legal and financial responsibility. This type of business doesn't protect you from liability and taxes are still pretty high.

General Partnership

This form of partnership is made up of two or more individuals who invest. You only pay taxes once, and there is still unlimited liability, which means all members of the partnership are collectively responsible for all of the company's acts and debts, as well as the actions of the other partners.

Limited Partnership (L.P.)

This is where a general partner teams with a partner with limited interest in the management of the business. The limited partner is not liable for debts and claims; however, the general partner is liable for all debts and claims against the business.

S Corporation & Limited Liability Company (L.L.C)

An S corporation is limited to 75 shareholders, while an L.L.C. (depending on the state) can have one or more owners referred to as "Members" with no maximum. These set-ups protect principals from legal and financial liabilitie,s and income is only taxed once, as all the profit passes through to your personal tax return.

C Corporation

C corporations protect shareholders from any liabilities and allow large earnings to be retained and reinvested in the growth of the business. However, income is taxed on the corporate level, then when it is disbursed to the shareholders, it is taxed again on their personal tax return.

Always consult a qualified accountant and an attorney to help you determine which structure is right for you.

More asset protection: Talk to your attorney about a trust or layered corporations. These can be another way to protect your assets. They essentially place assets outside the reach of creditors. However, nothing is ironclad, and it is essential to know all your options and potential ramifications of any strategy you use.

NOTE – Take a minute and jot down a few questions you want to ask your attorney about structures and asset protection. Don't HAVE an attorney yet? Don't worry – we'll work on that later in the section.

Insurance

Insurance plays an important role in protecting both you and your business. It protects you against liability and loss and helps to ensure that you don't have to pay for any incurred expenses out of your own personal bank account. Additionally, it helps to limit any claims against you.

Here are some items you may wish to carry insurance on:

- Equipment (e.g. computers, fax machines)

Lead

- Inventory
- Buildings, land or fixtures
- Liability
- Business interruption
- Vehicles registered to the business
- Any vehicle, even those owned by employees while being used in the business, or which your business temporarily uses

Management Exercise #12: Insurance Inventory

Take an inventory of items to be insured. Write down a list of what the items are, and then decide how much each is worth, should a loss occur. Be realistic. Once you know what you want to insure, decide what kind of coverage you need.

Now take that list, and make a separate list. What is it you would like to be protected from?

- Fire
- Theft
- Catastrophes
- Accidents
- Loss of Income/disability

Management Exercise #13: Go Shopping

Using the information you just compiled, begin searching for the right prices and insurance package for your personal and business needs. Much of this information can be found online, but it's better to just make an appointment with a reputable business insurance representative in your area. The education you will get is well worth the hour of your time.

Note: If you're running a home-based business, take a close look at your homeowner's policy. Most homeowner policies limit, or even exclude, coverage for any business-related equipment. This includes personal computers, fax machines, laptops, and inventory.

Protecting the BUSINESS' ASSets

Being a business owner requires a few basic steps to appease your local and federal government. Many of these steps revolve around income tax reporting, but a few steps help the government protect its citizens by making sure that all businesses are properly licensed.

Your first step is to register your business. Registering your business is a very straightforward process. There are several things you can do.

The first one, which we recommend, is contacting a trusted, recommended accountant – hopefully you already have one. Tell them about your type of business, and they will be able to advise you how to register your business. They can also take care of all the paperwork for you and keep copies of your records as well. It should only take about two weeks for the business to be registered.

Lead

Another option is to contact your local City Hall and fill out an application to register your business yourself. They will be able to advise you on the steps required. If you choose to open your business under a fictitious name or a name other than your own, it will take a little longer (not much) and cost a little more. A lot of people choose this option as they prefer to have a company name rather than using their own name for their business. We've already talked about the importance of keeping your business and personal life separate.

You will be given a fictitious business name license application which you fill in and send back. Your chosen name will be checked to make sure it's available and you'll soon be in business. In most places you can also check to see if your chosen name is available online before filling out the application and even apply online. Ask your local City Hall how to register online.

Visit the Small Business Associations' website: http://www.sba.gov/hotlist/license.html. Here you will find the registration requirements that apply to your state.

Your second step may be to obtain a business license. This depends largely on what type of business you're operating and where you live. For example, if you're a fitness coach you may need a license to operate. Check with your local government or the Small Business Bureau on what your state requirements are.

The next step is to obtain a tax id number. If you've created a business entity like an L.L.C., this is sometimes included in the process, depending on if someone is handling the process for you. If you're doing it yourself, visit http://www.irs.gov/businesses/small/article/0,,id=102767,00.html and you can obtain your EIN online.

What are the requirements for the type of entity you have? Make sure you know what your reporting requirements are. For example, a business owner is required to file quarterly tax payments to the IRS. Your accountant can guide you with estimating how much you will pay. This is important because if you don't pay these quarterly taxes, you could end up paying a penalty on top of your quarterly taxes – the IRS doesn't let anything slip by! State taxes may be the same. Is your company operating as a foreign entity? For example, did you decide to open up a Nevada corporation for privacy and asset protection, but you live in Georgia? Have you filed the proper documents with both states? And is everything up to date?

Management Exercise #14: Confirm Compliance

Go back through these steps, and make sure you're on top of everything and in compliance. Missing one date or piece of information could be expensive, and nobody wants to flush money down the toilet, especially not the government toilet.

US Tax Law Basics

Here's another area where it pays, literally, to be in compliance.

- Do you have to pay sales tax?
- Unemployment tax? (yes some states require this, even if you as the owner are the only employee)
- Withholding tax?

Lead

- Self-employment tax?

Even if you're not doing your accounting and taxes, it's important to know the rules. We're sure you know that if you're found to be delinquent in your taxes or the IRS deems you worthy of an audit, it isn't your accountant that will take the heat, it is you. So why oh why would you place 100% trust in one single person without understanding the rules of the game? Would you go onto a football field without knowing the rules of the game? It's a sure way to get clobbered. That being said, this isn't a course in business tax law. We're just covering the basics.

Writing it Off: Deductions

Such a scary area. Here's the lowdown. Businesses can deduct all "ordinary and necessary" business expenses from their revenues to reduce their taxable income.

Okay, so that wasn't much help. Let me ask you this. Your dog keeps your feet warm when you work from home, right? So feeding and caring for the dog is a deduction, right? NOT!

However, the laptop that is keeping your lap warm is, assuming you only use it for business.

While some deductions are obvious, like business travel, business equipment, salaries, and rent, others are more questionable. Here are a few potential deductions:

- Trips that combine business and pleasure. If a business trip is primarily devoted to business, you may deduct the travel costs and other business-related expenses.

- Purchases financed by business loans or credit cards. These costs can be deducted this year, even if they won't be paid off until later. Deduct the interest on the loans themselves as well.

- Start-up expenditures. Only a portion of expenses related to starting up a business can be deducted – $5,000 of general start-up costs, and $5,000 of organizational costs. Additional expenses must be amortized over 180 months once the company is up and running.

Always talk with your accountant about any deductions or potential deductions! We're not tax accountants, and we don't want to be responsible for your audit!

Employee Taxes

If your business has employees, a variety of taxes will have to be withheld from their salaries including:

- Withholding. Social Security (FICA), Medicare, and federal and state income taxes must be withheld from employees' pay.

- Employer matching. Businesses must match the FICA and Medicare taxes and pay them along with employees.

- Unemployment tax. Businesses must pay federal and state unemployment taxes.

Note – if you've hired an outsource employee, they're responsible for their own taxes, but you have to make sure

Lead

you document everything properly to prove that they really ARE an "independent contractor" rather than an employee (more on that in a bit).

Fun Tax Deadlines!

Your accountant should know these by heart. If they don't, find another accountant. However, it is also beneficial for you to know these dates so you can plan ahead.

- Annual returns.

- Due April 15 for unincorporated companies.

- Due March 15 for corporations with a calendar tax year.

- For corporations with a non-calendar fiscal year – due two and a half months after the end of the fiscal year.

- Estimated taxes. Due four times a year: April 15, June 15, September 15, and January 15.

- Sales taxes. Due quarterly or monthly, depending on the rules in your state.

- Employee taxes. Depending on the size of your payroll, employee taxes are due weekly, monthly, or quarterly.

Management Exercise #15: Fun with Taxes!

We're not going to beat around the bush here. Complying with the IRS is important. Remember what happened to that naked guy who won Survivor? He ended up getting charged with tax evasion and spending time in jail. Not a fun way to spend your hard-earned millions! Consider the following, and make a list of any actions you need to take to ensure you are in compliance with IRS requirements and regulations.

- Where are you complying?

- What, if any, areas will you be investigating to ensure compliance?

- How will you ensure compliance?

Contracts

This is a word that is almost as scary as taxes to some business owners. Contracts don't have to be major formal affairs all the time, and can and should be written in CLEAR English, but EVERY agreement should be documented and done in writing.

Contractors have very different contracts to sign than employees. Outsourcing contracts will cover the following basics:

- Confidentiality. What can and cannot be said about a company. For example, a ghostwriter cannot post on their website that they ghostwrote the Amazon #1 Bestseller and name the book. Not if they don't want to get sued.

- Rights. Who owns what after the project is accomplished. Again, using the ghostwriter example, does the book now belong 100% to the employer or does the writer retain any rights? Usually the answer is no.

- Service Terms. What are the parameters of the project? For example, that a ghostwriter will complete a book on pet care by said date.

- Description. What is the description of the project?

- Payment terms. How is the contractor going to be paid?

- Communication terms. How will both parties communicate?

Employee agreements are a bit different. While they will also have a job description, and many have a confidentiality clause, they will also outline the salary, bonuses, incentives, benefits, termination policies, non-compete, and review or evaluation policies.

Management Exercise #16: Check Out Contracts

Find a sample contract, for both an outsourced employee and an in-house hire, if you don't already have one, and keep it on file.

Employee Law vs. Contractor Law

According to the IRS, an Independent Contractor is defined by the following: "A general rule is that you, the payer, have the right to control or direct only the result of the work done by an independent contractor, and not the means and methods of accomplishing the result."

An employee is defined as: "A general rule is that anyone who performs services for you is your employee if you can control what will be done and how it will be done."

So how does that affect your business? When you hire an employee, you're responsible for their safety while they're on the job. You also have certain guidelines in respect to your employee's privacy – though not many. We're not going to get into the basics of the law and monitoring employees in this lesson. Ask your lawyer..

Management Exercise #17: Hire an Attorney

Hire an attorney to ensure you're in compliance, to establish your business entity if you haven't already and to ensure your business and your personal assets are protected via insurance and other asset protection strategies. You may choose to go with either a firm or an individual; however, consider that firms are generally better able to handle your different needs because they employ attorneys with many areas of specialty. And they usually aren't significantly more expensive. Just like you wouldn't go to your general practice doctor if you needed brain surgery, you don't go to a general practice attorney to handle a multi-tiered asset protection plan or a business asset sale.

If you already have an attorney, set up a meeting to ensure you're in compliance.

Lead

Write a list of questions to ask an attorney. Here's a short list to get you started:

- How long have you been practicing law?

- What is your area of specialty?

- Have you represented companies like mine and for what?

- Who are the attorneys and paralegals at your firm that would work on my matters, and what experience do they have?

- How do you charge legal fees, and do you require a retainer?

- Do you have sample legal forms, agreements, and policies that I can use for my business?

- How many corporations have you incorporated?

- What experience do you have in handling employment matters?

- What experience do you have in dealing with tax matters?

- What kinds of advice do you give to businesses to lessen the likelihood of litigation?

- What type of organizational structure is best for my business?

- I'm outsourcing. What information do I need to know to protect myself?

- I'm hiring employees. What information do I need to know to protect myself?

Documents to bring to your first meeting:

- A business plan or summary of information about your business.

- A balance sheet, including assets and liabilities that are going to be contributed to or assumed by any business entity.

- A list of investors or directors in your business. Tax returns, financial statements, or corporate records for your business.

- Any agreements, minutes of meetings, or notes relating to the organization of the business.

- Letters, memos, or other correspondence relating to the business.

- A diagram or organizational chart of your business.

Inspired Action

Here's where we pull it all together and put it into action. This is the feel-good moment of the guide. True, you already feel good about what you've accomplished, but here is where you plan for the future based on what you've just accomplished. Take some time, just a bit, and fill out the inspired-action SMART Plans. Then, just before you close the book, repeat the evaluation you took at the beginning. Taking one look back at all you've accomplished will give you a great feeling.

Go back through your notes, worksheets, and exercises, and list all of your targets, goals, and action steps:

- What steps are you going to take to hire your next employee? What tools will you use?

- What steps will you take to ensure you're in compliance both financially and legally going forward?

- How often will you evaluate both your personal and business finances?

- What systems do you need to put into place to make your business more productive?

List one item per line and after you have them all listed, rank each one in order of priority. Rank the one that will make the biggest impact in your business and your life RIGHT NOW as number 1, the second as number 2 and so on down the list.

Take the top three, and create a SMART Plan for each one. Work those plans until you hit the target, then come back, and create a SMART Plan for the next three. Remember, SMART plans must include:

S – pecific

M – easurable

A – ttainable

R – ealistic

T – ime Trackable

Lead

What's Your Management Score NOW?

When you've completed this evaluation, compare the score to the first time you took it. You may be surprised how much you've changed in the short time it's taken you to complete the guide.

On a scale of 1-10 (10 being the highest), rank where you currently stand with regard to the management of your business.

I know what areas of the business I need help with and have a plan for bringing that help in.

1   2   3   4   5   6   7   8   9   10

I know how to create comprehensive job descriptions, listings and SOPs to assist in hiring and training new team members.

1   2   3   4   5   6   7   8   9   10

I understand the differences between outsourcing and hiring, and know which option is best for my business right now.

1   2   3   4   5   6   7   8   9   10

I'm confident in my ability to evaluate candidates for a position in my company.

1   2   3   4   5   6   7   8   9   10

I have a step-by-step system for interviewing candidates and their references.

1   2   3   4   5   6   7   8   9   10

I am confident that my personal and business finances are in order, and I have people and systems in place to ensure they stay that way.

1   2   3   4   5   6   7   8   9   10

I know the most important systems in my business and have metrics in place to measure their effectiveness and performance.

1   2   3   4   5   6   7   8   9   10

I am confident that my personal and business assets are being protected.

1   2   3   4   5   6   7   8   9   10

I am confident that my business is compliant on all local, state, and federal tax and licensing issues.

SCORING

Add up all the numbers you circled._____

Divide the total number by 9

Record your NEW "Management Score" here _____

Lead

Did you see an improvement in your score? Why do you think you did or did not?

Come back in a month, six months, or even a year and retake the assessment to see how your knowledge and use of your business strategy has changed your business outcomes.

Conclusion

Whew! Finishing this guide is a major achievement! If you look back on all you've accomplished, you'll see it was worth the time and effort.

You've hired a new employee, you've met with your accountant and your attorney to make sure you're 100% in compliance and that there will be no unexpected knocks on your door by any government official.

You've insured yourself and protected your assets.

You know where your finances stand, both personal and business.

You've established systems to make getting things accomplished easy and repeatable, and you've created a few metrics to make sure your systems are working the way you want them to.

What now?

Now breathe, relax, and celebrate. Give yourself an enormous pat on the back and take an afternoon off, or even a weekend getaway. Just revel in the glory and satisfaction of having set up a comprehensive management system. You're ahead of 99% of the business owners out there.

Now it's time to take what you have learned and make a difference in your business.

Lead

Remember, management is about being able to see the big picture and then taking the action necessary to turn your dreams into reality!

Ric Thompson

Ric Thompson

Check out some of Ric's other books!!

http://www.amazon.com/dp/B00I3Q2QPK

http://www.amazon.com/dp/B00LIGKRCG

Lead

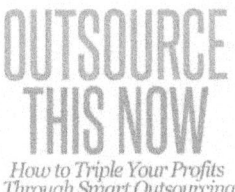

http://www.amazon.com/dp/B00H4HHY56

http://www.amazon.com/dp/B00L9K6928

www.ingramcontent.com/pod-product-compliance
Lightning Source LLC
Chambersburg PA
CBHW051735170526
45167CB00002B/939